The Hidden Heart Series
"Beauty"

Copyright © 2014 by Cindy Dahl
All rights reserved
www.cindydahl2007.wordpress.com

Art by Shaun Crum

ISBN-13: 978-1-941030-05-9

BEAUTY

By Cindy Dahl

Illustrated By Shaun Crum

Hi, I am a GLíCK®. You say it like /glēk/.
It stands for Giving, Loving, Inspiring, Caring
and Kind. My books will show you how to be
a GLíCK just like me!
I have hidden a heart in one of the pages;
see if you can find the love in this book.

Hint: The hidden heart is in a field of flowers.

Seeing something beautiful
Makes you feel good inside.
Whether it's a person
Or the ocean's tide.

Think of how you feel
When you watch it snow.
It can get exciting,
It's such a beautiful show.

You ever watch the sun
When it sets down in the sky?
The beauty of the colors
Can be fantastic, that's no lie.

There is beauty in nature
That can take your breath away.
From the waters, to the mountains,
To the birds that fly all day.

After a big rain
A rainbow may appear.
Rainbows are so beautiful
You'll always want them here.

Even storms can offer beauty.
A lighting show is hard to beat,
As long as you are safe
And not standing in the street.

Billowing clouds offer beauty
Especially with different shapes.
Some clouds look like dogs
While others look like Apes.

There is nothing like camping
With a beautiful campfire.
You can roast a marshmallow
Or a hotdog on a wire.

Animals are beautiful
We like to watch them play.
It brings joy to our hearts
And brightens up our day.

Even a simple act
Like holding open a door,
Is a beautiful thing to do
And shouldn't be a chore.

People can have beauty
Like pretty eyes or hair,
But still may not be beautiful
If they don't seem to care.

Treating people nicely
Is the only way to be.
This is beauty from the inside
That you can't really see.

You may have heard the saying
That "beauty is skin deep."
That just because someone's pretty,
They're not a friend you'd want to kee

"Beauty is not in the face; beauty is a light in the heart."

— Kahlil Gibran

    Cindy Dahl is the author of several feel good children's books including the entire "hidden heart series" where kids get to find the hidden heart in each book. "It's like finding the love in the pages of a book." Cindy's main goal with writing her books is to inspire and bring a positive message for kids at a very young age. "It is never too young to learn to be kind to one another, to feel good about yourself, and to share with others."

    Cindy grew up on a farm in Northern California and currently resides in Colorado. Cindy has three grown children. She read to them often when they were young and loved watching their faces when they felt the story come alive. In her spare time, Cindy enjoys being in the great Colorado outdoors.